I don't
know

ALSO BY LEAH HAGER COHEN

I don't know

IN PRAISE OF ADMITTING IGNORANCE

(Except When You Shouldn't)

Leah Hager Cohen

RIVERHEAD BOOKS

A MEMBER OF PENGUIN GROUP (USA)

NEW YORK

2013

RIVERHEAD BOOKS
Published by the Penguin Group
Penguin Group (USA) LLC, 375 Hudson Street,
New York, New York 10014, USA

USA · Canada · UK · Ireland · Australia
New Zealand · India · South Africa · China

penguin.com
A Penguin Random House Company

Library of Congress Cataloging-in-Publication Data

Cohen, Leah Hager.
I don't know : in praise of admitting ignorancet
(except when you shouldn't) / Leah Hager Cohen.
p.   cm.
ISBN 978-1-59463-239-6
1. Truthfulness and falsehood.   2. Ignorance (Theory of
knowledge)   3. Skepticism.   I. Title.
BJ1421.C64   2013   2013024605
177'.3—dc23

Printed in the United States of America
1   3   5   7   9   10   8   6   4   2

BOOK DESIGN BY AMANDA DEWEY

A few identifying details have been changed in order
to preserve the privacy of those who wished it.

to

Mary Page
(who knew?)

"I do not know" is a phrase which becomes us.

JEAN-JACQUES ROUSSEAU

I don't
know

One

L et's look at the prison piece," said the professor. "What does the nut graph tell us?"

Around me rose a soft rustle as other students
rifled knowledgeably through the photocopied
news stories we'd been given at the start of class.
I found the article on inmate crowding, but as I
turned its pages, failed to spot anything that might
fit the professor's specification. I looked at first
for something acorn-shaped, then for anything
vaguely pictorial, but could find no pie chart, no
bar graph, no pyramid diagram—nary an illustra-
tion in the entire piece. I glanced around. Everyone
else seemed to have managed the task; they sat

absorbedly regarding their copies of the article while the professor continued, parsing the information apparently contained within this elusive "nut graph." What page were they all on? I strained to see, but couldn't get an angle. How distinctly I remember growing damp then, my skin flocked with sweat.

I was twenty-two and in my first week of graduate school in journalism. I knew by their appearances that most of my classmates were older, just as I knew from the school's brochure, which promised to provide journalists "a unique opportunity to hone and deepen their skills at any point in their careers," that many of them already had experience working in the field, whereas I had never so much as written for my college newspaper. But until the moment I searched in vain for the devilish little entity called a nut graph, I'd been more thrilled than cowed, eagerly optimistic about joining their ranks.

Now I sat awash in shame. It wasn't the shame of incompetence so much as the shame of hubris. To think I had dared imagine I could be a journalist! I couldn't even keep up with the class in the very first week of instruction.

Did I raise my hand to ask for help? Turn to a neighbor with whispered appeal?

I did not. The cost felt too great. To confess my ignorance would be to expose my inadequacy; I would be cast off, dismissed from this world to which I craved entry. Such was my fear, and it was powerful enough to make stewing in the solitary confinement of my shame seem a preferable alternative.

In time I would learn that "nut graph" is, in fact, "nut graf" (*graf* being journalism slang for *paragraph*) and refers to that part of an article, usually following the lead, that gives a condensed overview of its news value. In time I would discover that I was, after all, up to the task of successfully completing the course of study. In time, as I incrementally proved my worth to myself and others, I would even find the courage to speak up, on occasion, when I came across something I did not understand.

But the memory of that first class more than two decades ago remains uncomfortably sharp. Its residue of fear and shame has never entirely dissipated. And I still sometimes struggle with saying "I don't know."

. . .

Fakery is a vital currency in our social intercourse. That's not necessarily all bad. A lot of
the time we pretend as a way of fortifying or easing
connections. When we feign recognition, for example, or delight in seeing someone, or gladness to
go out of our way, these are acts of goodwill. At
best, pretense can be a form of kindness.

But the benign desire to spare ourselves
and others embarrassment or disappointment or
pain can lead to actions that engender greater falsehood, promulgate more fear. How easily we fall
into the pattern of using deception as a shield
against feeling uncomfortable. At worst, it can breed
a habit of shirking responsibility and avoiding
vulnerability—behaviors that ultimately distance
us from the very prizes we crave: true connection
with others and integrity within ourselves.

This book looks at two kinds of pretending:
pretending to know stuff we don't, and pretending
not to know stuff we do—for just as we might avoid
saying "I don't know" for fear of being ridiculed or
rejected, the flip can also be true: Sometimes we
pretend ignorance of things we think might lower

our cachet, whether to prove our membership in highbrow culture ("What's a Kardashian?") or to accommodate social pressures (as so many women of my mother's generation were warned, "Boys aren't attracted to smart girls").

This book also looks at two kinds of fear: fear of estrangement and fear of stepping into the abyss—for as much as we might worry that saying "I don't know" could cost us the human company we desire, evict us from our place around the hearth, there's an even more primal fear associated with not knowing: that our inability to comprehend the universe might threaten our very survival. Our efforts to compensate for both social and psychic fears manifest in some pretty interesting ways.

Finally, this book looks at two kinds of hope: that which comes from opening ourselves up to a greater understanding of the world and ourselves and that which comes from making peace with all that must, in the end, remain unknown.

In August 2012, Harvard University announced it was investigating allegations that approximately 125 undergraduates taking an Introduction to Congress class had cheated on the take-home final the previous spring. In December 2012, the investigation concluded with more than half those students being forced to withdraw. The dean of undergraduate education described the case as "unprecedented in its scope and magnitude." The press quickly dubbed it "the Harvard cheating scandal."

A scandal is something that causes outrage and shock, reactions which in this case were likely exacerbated by a perceived discrepancy between the actors and the behavior. Those who succumbed to the temptation to cheat had already gained admittance to one of the most elite educational institutions in the world. The subtext of much of the resultant furor seemed to be, "But you guys are already in. You guys have it made. Of all people, why would *you* guys feel the need to cheat?"

This presupposes that the very smart are also the very emotionally secure—that they never feel intense pressure to prove their worth or to save face. But surely such weaknesses are human; who among us has never felt vulnerable to them? And I further wonder if those who have been granted the measure of approval signaled by acceptance into a competitive school might actually be *more* susceptible to certain anxieties. I'm thinking of the way college students sometimes contort their prose into incomprehensibly pretentious muddles, all in a disastrous bid to sound erudite. I'm thinking of the way junior faculty may blush pink to the rims of their ears as they struggle to cover for lack of familiarity with a text or theory mentioned by a senior scholar. I'm thinking of the subtly stratifying culture prevalent on many college campuses, not only in the classroom but at the water cooler and on the quad, a kind of endless cycle of proving and testing, of esoteric referencing and faked recognition, a game played out in grimaces and knowing nods belied by a look of vague panic in the eyes.

My friend Gary tells this joke:

A high school senior from the Bronx is
visiting Harvard. Lost, he intercepts a
young man striding across the Yard.
"Excuse me," he says, "could you
please tell me where the library's at?"

The young man peers down his nose.
"Here at Harvard," he edifies, "we never
end our sentences with a preposition."

The kid scrunches his brow, thinks

earnestly a moment. "Excuse me," he says, "could you please tell me where the library's at, asshole?"

I don't submit such snooty gatekeeping is either the norm or the whole story. But if there weren't a crumb of truth in it, the joke wouldn't exist.

People cheat when they are afraid. When there is no cost to being wrong or confessing ignorance, there is no reason to cheat or fake comprehension. During my first week of graduate school, fear kept me from asking what a nut graph is. As I grew more confident, both of my skills and of my relationships with classmates and professors, my fear diminished and, with it, the compulsion to pretend I understood.

When I heard about the Harvard cheating scandal, I cannot say I was particularly scandalized. It didn't shock me to imagine students being afraid of getting it wrong, coming up short, revealing their weaknesses. So much of education is premised on the value of displaying knowledge. If a student displays well, she is rewarded—initially with grades and later with opportunities: promotion to the next level, acceptance to prestigious programs, and the promise of financial success, social capital, happiness. If a student displays inadequately, if she baldly confesses, "I don't know," she may find her access to these opportunities restricted. No wonder students are often fearful of acknowledging what they haven't yet mastered—or simply don't get.

Colleges realize that breaches of academic integrity present an important problem on campuses today. Many now require instructors to address the topic outright on the first day of class. I've taught at schools where I've been asked to do this. Dutifully, I've reviewed the handbook with students, rehearsing with them what constitutes plagiarism and cheating, and identifying the consequences of each. During this, the students' eyes seem to flicker with resentment and anxiety: the former triggered by finding themselves subjected to disciplinary *tsk*ings before they so much as uncap their pens; the latter triggered by being asked to envision how easily, unless they maintain constant vigilance, they risk morphing into perpetrators of these crimes.

Talk about starting the semester on a high note.

I didn't like it any more than the students. And I couldn't help feeling we were tiptoeing around the underlying issue. If cheating and plagiarism are caused by fear, wouldn't it make sense to talk about *that*?

So I stopped going over the official policies with students and started telling them instead about my friend Mary.

"My friend Mary," I say, "is the bravest person I know. She taught English for ages, three or four decades. She's really well-read, incredibly smart. But what makes her so uncommonly brave is what she does when she's having a conversation and the other person mentions a book or author in that way that assumes she's familiar with the work." I look around the classroom. "You know what I'm talking about, right?"

They look back blankly.

"You know when you're with people you want to impress, people you find a little intimidating? Maybe you're feeling kind of dumb, like you don't really belong with them. You're worried you'll be found out. And somebody mentions a writer or the title of a book in this tone like, *Naahh-turally you know what I'm talking about.* And even though you have no clue, you do that little thing where you narrow your eyes and purse your lips and give this thoughtful nod."

By now some of the students are grinning; a few nod their own heads knowingly.

"You know what Mary does in that situation?"

They're quiet, alert.

"She says, 'I don't know that book.' She says, 'I've never heard of that person.'"

Sometimes here one or two students will laugh—not so much because they find it funny, I think, as out of pure relief. Every shoulder in the room settles an inch.

"The first time I ever witnessed Mary do that," I continue, "I swore to myself I'd follow her example, I'd be that brave. Guess how I've done?"

They raise their eyebrows, half hopeful, half leery.

"Not that great," I confess. "It's ridiculous! I still do it sometimes! Less often, but yes—from time to time, I still catch myself faking it!"

Then I ask them why they think this is.

And so we talk about fear—their fear, mine, all of ours. We lay it out on the seminar table: the big, heavy animal body of our collective fear. It's usually sleeping by then, so we're able to talk freely, prod it a little, rearrange its tail, even stroke its fur and comb out some of the mats. We talk about which environments tend to feed it, in which situations we feel most at its mercy. We notice that academia is one of its natural habitats, and we discuss what we can do to make our own environment less hospitable to it. We pledge to start by committing to bravery in the tradition of Mary; we pledge, at least within the enclosure of our classroom, to own our limits without apology, to be forthright about what knowledge we lack.

Whence this fear? Were we born with it?
Ashley Montagu, the twentieth-century anthropologist* and humanist, thought not. In *Growing Young*, his 1989 book on human development, he singled out curiosity as one of the most conspicuous traits of children, along with playfulness, candor, and a propensity to experiment and to try again upon failing. While celebrating children's

---

* Incidentally (and wonderfully), in American Sign Language the sign for anthropology, the study of humanity, is a cognate of the sign for I-don't-know.

lack of fear, he made clear that knowledge gathering isn't all fun and games. "The need to know," he wrote, "is a first-order evolutionary drive—vital for survival and development." Montagu saw this drive declaring itself within hours of birth, evident in the way an infant makes eye contact with his mother, scanning her face, already absorbing information by which to organize his raw sensations. This drive, he said, is what fuels children's explorations and their endless, unabashed questions: "Why?" "What is it?" "What's it for?"

Over time, he lamented, we lose our openness. Montagu attributed this in part to conventional schooling, which he blamed for squashing a love of knowledge. "School, instead of being a magic casement which opens on unending vistas of excitement, has become a restrictive, linear, one-dimensional, only too often narrowing, experience and to many a dead loss." By the time formal education stops, around early adulthood for most people, "it is as though they believed that they had learned all they needed to know," he wrote. "At this time they begin to grow a shell around this pitiful store of knowledge and wisdom; from then on they vigorously resist all attempts to pierce that shell with anything new." Montagu called this process psychosclerosis, the hardening of the mind, and cited it as the reason that most adults "draw back from the unfamiliar, perhaps because they are reluctant to reveal ignorance."

But might such reluctance actually start much earlier?

Just the other day my ten-year-old niece, Abby, shared an experience she had in school:

> My math teacher asked me why I wasn't raising my hand, so I admitted I didn't know the answer. So then he pulled me out of the room and started yelling and screaming at me because I didn't know the answer to a question. Then he started going on and *on* about how I am one of "the top kids in the class" and it lasted for about twenty minutes to half an hour. I went back into the class red-faced.

What kills me is the detail "it lasted for about twenty minutes to half an hour." One suspects this may not be, strictly speaking, accurate. But what a wonderfully accurate representation of how it must have *felt*.

I don't know

A week or so later, I asked Abby how things were going. She replied:

The bottom line is: MR. B HAS RUINED MATH FOR ME!!! I'm sick of it! I used to love math! But now it's just another lousy school period.

After careful consideration, she has decided the best course of action henceforth is to conceal any confusion she might experience in class, instead taking her questions home to her mother (who, by a stroke of luck, happens to be a middle-school math teacher).

In this story, we see a ten-year-old receiving a clear message that openly confessing "I don't know" carries the consequence of being actively shamed. But children are capable of grasping the disadvantages of not knowing even younger than this, and without such overt cues.

My partner, Mike, teaches kindergarten in a Boston public school. Part of his job involves evaluating each of his students' early reading skills, specifically letter identification. Invariably, he gets one or two kids with whom the process goes like this:

Mike: I'm going to point to a letter of the alphabet, and if you know what it is, tell me. If you don't, that's fine—just say "I don't know." Okay?

Kid: *(Nods.)*

Mike: Okay. *(Shows her a sheet printed with all the letters of the alphabet, out of sequence. He points to one.)* You know what this is?

Kid: *(Nods.)*

Mike: What is it?

Kid: . . .

Mike: You don't know? That's okay. Remember, if you don't know, just say "I don't know." Okay?

Kid: *(Nods.)*

Mike: Okay. *(Points to another letter.)* Do you know what this is?

Kid: *(Nods.)*

Mike: What is it?

Kid: . . .

Even when encouraged to tell the truth, even when given a demonstration of how to do it, some children just can't shake the idea that admitting not knowing is bad. It seems we are capable, whether or not we've had a particular shaming experience, of incorporating this belief at a very young age. A childhood friend who excelled in school and always struck me as the quintessence of confidence recently told me he never learned to ride a bike. His parents tried to teach him when he was small. When he couldn't get the hang of it right away, he rejected all further entreaties. Reflecting on it now, he gives a rueful laugh: "I was a child who hated to learn anything I didn't already know."

Another friend, a psychotherapist, recounts how her grandson would often cut in with "I know!" whenever she began to tell him something. "As a little boy," she muses, "he was particularly sensitive to his lack of power vis-à-vis grown-ups."

This seems right. Children are acutely attuned to power, the desire for which long precedes their ability to articulate it. I once witnessed the following interaction:

My daughter, not yet three, stood on the playground, wistfully eying a pair of metal climbing bars that, as she had just discovered, were not quite within her reach. She could run her fingers along them, but couldn't manage a solid enough grip to

leah hager cohen

hoist herself up. A taller boy wandered over. He watched as she made another futile attempt to grab on and then, with a degree of calculated insouciance I could not help but admire, raised himself onto the bars, where he swung pendulously a moment, as if making a point, before dropping back onto the wood chips.

"I'm four," he boasted, casually wiping off his hands.

Unfazed, my daughter shot back: "I'm six."

My jaw, as I recall, literally dropped. I'm not sure which surprised me more: the fact that she was sufficiently numerate, at age two, to have sussed out that six was greater than four, or the ease with which she'd dissimulated, as if she'd been lying all her life. I was also, perhaps perversely, rather proud, or at least gladdened to see that she was loath to accept a position of inferiority. But what strikes me most about the story now (Ashley Montagu's belief in the receptivity and truthfulness of children notwithstanding) is that she had already, at such a tender age, developed a rudimentary awareness of the desirability of power and authority—for in laying claim to being six, wasn't she countering the boy's physical prowess by implying vast stores of knowledge she held over him?—as well as an instinct for using dishonesty as a means of asserting them.

That our aversion to not knowing is both age-old and primal seems borne out by a couple of fairy tales.

The first is Hans Christian Andersen's "The Emperor's New Clothes," originally published in Denmark in 1837, although it can be traced back as far as ancient Persia and appears in different versions all over the world, including in Sri Lanka, Turkey, India, Spain, Germany, and China. The story tells of a sartorially vain emperor who proves an easy target for two swindlers who promise to weave him the finest cloth imaginable—a material not only beautiful but magical, too, for it would be "invisible to anyone who was incompetent or stupid." The swindlers set up their empty looms and pretend to get to work. The emperor, curious to know how things are coming along, but (presciently) wary of going to see for himself, sends his top minister to visit the workroom. Of course the minister cannot spot so much as a thread, but afraid of being exposed as stupid, he reports back to the emperor that the fabric is magnificent. Subsequently the emperor sends more officials to observe; each in turn expounds on the cloth's glories. Plans are made to hold a grand procession so the entire city can view the emperor in his splendid new suit.

The day comes. The swindlers "dress" the emperor in the imaginary garments with great care and attention to detail, even indicating the long train that must be carried by his chamberlains. The emperor beholds his naked body in the mirror and expresses admiration of the nonexistent ensemble. The procession begins. People line the streets and lean out of their windows, all proclaiming loud words of praise as the emperor passes, lest they be thought stupid. At last a small child cries, "But he doesn't have anything on!"

One by one, the people repeat the words of the child until they reach even the ears of the emperor, who shudders in recognition of their truth. We feel sorry for him, a little. But he has been so pompous and preening, and after all, he holds both power and wealth. When such a man loses face, it's an occasion more for humor than pity. And as if to prove that he deserves our derision, the last we see of him he's still stubbornly clinging to pretense. For he insists on continuing the parade—and charade. The story ends, "He carried himself even more proudly, and the chamberlains walked along behind carrying the train that wasn't there."

The second, much darker, tale is from Germany: the Grimm Brothers' "Rumpelstiltskin," originally published in 1812. This story, too, crops up in many different forms in many other countries, among them England, Wales, Ireland, Scotland, Sweden, Austria, Italy, and Hungary. And it begins, like "The Emperor's New Clothes," with an act of vanity: A miller, wanting to make himself seem important, tells the king his daughter can spin straw into gold. But where the emperor's vanity results in humiliation, the miller's threatens consequences far more dire. The king promptly locks the girl in a room filled with straw and a spinning wheel, informing her the straw must be turned to gold by morning or her head will be chopped off.

Now lack of knowledge is a matter of life and death. She could choose to confess "I don't know how," but the cost would be her life. Hopeless, she begins to weep. When a strange little man appears, offering to complete the task for her, she has little choice but to agree—and to keep up the sham of false know-how when the king returns at dawn. This pattern is repeated the next night, and the next, and each time the miller's daughter is forced not only to maintain the lie that it's her own handiwork but also to succumb to the stranger's demand for payment, which on the third night consists of the unthinkable: her firstborn child.

The king marries her. A year later she gives birth. Promptly the strange little man shows up, prepared to cart the baby off. The miller's daughter protests so piteously that he relents: If she can find out his name, he will let her keep her infant. Once more, a seemingly impossible test. Once more, she is in frantic need of knowledge she does not possess. And where in the first instance her life was at stake, this time the cost is even higher.

Never mind that it ends happily for the miller's daughter. "Rumpelstiltskin" is a chilling tale, not simply because it traffics in death threats and baby snatching, but because it so expertly evokes the terror of what it could mean to lack knowledge. In a sense, the two fairy tales illuminate the full spectrum of our fears about our own ignorance. On one end, Andersen shows us the relatively benign hazard of embarrassment, while on the other, the Grimms evoke the hellish specter of death and worse.

And they do more than illuminate: They inculcate. For these tales aren't mere relics, reflective of the cultures in which they originated; they're alive and well today, being handed down to new generations of children. It's part of what we teach, right up there with "brush your teeth" and "say the pledge" and "know the multiplication tables": We teach the fear of looking dumb.

One of our best defenses against fear is humor, and humor makes excellent fodder of our fear of not knowing. Little wonder, then, that two stock characters in comedy are the know-it-all and the fool. How we love to see the former brought low and the latter emerge triumphant! The beginnings of this cathartic tradition extend so far back as to be untraceable. Take the commedia dell'arte, for example, which originated in sixteenth-century

Rome but may have antecedents in antiquity. It features a cast of stock characters, several of whom—the swaggering *Capitano*, the pompous *Dottore*, and *Pantalone*, the miserly merchant—fit the archetype of the powerful know-it-all lording it over the common folk, while their inevitable comeuppance is brought about by the deceptively hapless *zanni*, or servants: the fools.

The joke of the fool hinges on reversal. As Touchstone says in *As You Like It*, "The fool doth think he is wise, but the wise man knows himself to be a fool." The point can be made subtly enough to elude notice of the king, his court—everyone but the grinning audience. Or the point can be deliciously crude. Think slapstick: banana peels underfoot, pies in the face. Think of the Keystone Kops, those fabulously incompetent bulwarks of society, forever getting knocked down by little dogs, dragged through the dirt, muddied in puddles. Think of classic comedy teams—Laurel and Hardy, say, or Abbott and Costello—who capitalized on the pleasurable anticipation of seeing a smug straight man lose his composure to an indefatigably bumbling clown. Think of Wallace

Shawn's self-described genius Vizzini in *The Princess Bride*, who utters a last, scathing, "You fool!" to the Man in Black moments before outsmarting himself to death, or André the Giant's supposedly dim-witted Fezzik in the same movie, whose gentle dignity and resilience help save the day.

When we laugh at these situations where high status is exchanged for low, where pillars of confidence crumble and humble innocents prevail, are we merely experiencing schadenfreude, pleasure derived from the misfortune of others (albeit officious, even despotic others)? Surely that's part of it, and it's a little sobering to think our hilarity might be proportional to the degree of injury we carry around—that our delight in seeing the know-it-all fall might be commensurate with just how much we've felt kicked around by similar types.

But I believe something else is at work here as well, something that lifts our laughter beyond sadistic enjoyment and lends it a more generous, giddy dimension. To be toppled off the foundation of one's certainties can be distressing. It can also be a gift. Think of Steve Carell's Michael Scott in *The Office*, who manages to embody both know-it-all and fool in a single high-strung package. Regularly we see him—most often after a fall from dignity—experience flashes of insight and empathy, not infrequently accompanied by a smile of real sweetness, eyes sparkling with real tears. The fullness of our laughter in such cases may be an expression of this unspoken understanding: that to come into contact with a fool, whether in the person of another or the fool within, can be an opportunity for transcendence. "Shakespeare's fools are subtle teachers," writes the scholar Mark Edmundson. "They tickle, coax, and cajole their supposed betters into truth . . . To be assigned a fool in Shakespeare is often a sign that one is, potentially, wise."

There's an old story in my family about the halls of academe, in which an entire class, belittled for its ignorance, finds a way to transform stinging shame into freeing laughter:

My parents met as graduate students, training to become teachers of the deaf. Their course on language development was taught by a famously irascible professor. One day she was lecturing about various theorists and linguists; it was all Vygotsky-this and Chomsky-that, and then she made reference to Hayakawa. She must have sensed a shift in the air, a little vacuum of unrecognition, for she stopped lecturing and narrowed her eyes at the class.

"You all know Hayakawa."

No response.

Again, more peevishly: "You all know Hayakawa."

No response.

"Who *doesn't* know Hayakawa?"

The class sat frozen, united in awkward ignorance.

"Well," she said after a protracted silence, and clicked her tongue. "If you don't know, I'm certainly not going to tell you."

This became an oft-repeated punch line, first among the cohort of students, and later within our family. I grew up hearing my parents repeat it in plummy tones, and we kids savored the sheer absurdity of the line long before we learned the story that accompanied it. The professor had sought to shame her students (by repeating the question when the answer was obvious) and wielded her power to punish them (by refusing to elucidate, withholding her knowledge). Yet in time the students used humor to defang the incident. At the end of the year they put on a variety show. In one of the skits, my father, bewigged and in drag, played the role of the tetchy professor, in which he answered all manner of questions ("Where's the bathroom?" "What time is it?" "How are you?") with the inevitable, now comic, refrain.

Two

Sometimes fear of not knowing has nothing to do with saving face or impressing others. It has to do with decision making and the anxiety that racks us when we must make an important choice in the absence of adequate knowledge. That anxiety is especially pronounced when we suspect none of the alternatives is especially attractive. The novelist Jane Smiley, writing of her quandary over whether to divorce the father of her two daughters, put it in memorably stark terms: "The choice of staying or leaving presented itself to me as a choice between suicide and mass murder."

Years ago my friend Will was caught in a similar dilemma. Will found himself in a marriage so unhappy, it threatened his emotional and physical well-being. But he could not shake the conviction that ending the relationship would be monstrous—tantamount to destroying the lives of his wife and children. Shouldn't he stay and make the best of it for their sakes? Or was that a fallacy? What if doing so actually sabotaged his wife's chances of experiencing a true connection with someone else? What if it imprinted his children with such a negative model of marriage that it jeopardized their chances for future partnered happiness? He kept weighing the pros and cons, hoping for a sign, and when none came, lapsed into fantasies about coming down with a fatal disease—any means of exiting the marriage that would absolve him of choosing.

His was a crisis of not knowing—or of knowing two contradictory things. He knew enough not to dismiss his feeling that the marriage was doomed. And he knew enough not to put blind trust in the certainty that he should leave. And for a long time, those impeccably counterbalanced items of knowledge kept him impeccably, miserably inert.

One day Will happened to see a television show about pararescue jumpers, or PJs. PJs are United States Air Force Special Operatives who perform unconventional, high-risk combat missions, like flying behind enemy lines to rescue downed pilots, and humanitarian work, like recovering civilians from the middle of the desert, the jungle, the wreckage of natural disasters, that kind of thing. They go through a two-year training program nicknamed Superman School, which is so arduous, it has a dropout rate of 90 percent—the highest dropout rate of any Special Ops program. This television show focused on the PJs made famous in Sebastian Junger's *The Perfect Storm: A True Story of Men Against the Sea.*

As Junger describes, they had flown out over the Atlantic in an H-60 Air National Guard helicopter in an attempt to save a civilian on a sinking sailboat when they ran out of fuel and had to ditch. The two PJs on board, Rick Smith and John Spillane, following protocol, assembled their survival gear and squatted near the open door of the helicopter. In his book, Junger likens the surface of the ocean to "a lunar landscape, cratered and gouged and deformed by wind." The water is so churned up "that they can't even tell the difference between the waves and the troughs; for all they know they are jumping three hundred feet." In other words,

Smith and Spillane knew that the timing of their jump would mean the difference between life and death. They also knew that in those conditions, the timing was incalculable.

Smith jumped. A split second later, Spillane followed. Spillane fell about seventy feet before he hit the water, fracturing an arm, a leg, four ribs, rupturing a kidney, and bruising his pancreas. He spent hours hanging on to a life raft before eventually being picked up by the Coast Guard. Smith was never found. It's possible that in the fragmentary interval between jumps, the surface of the ocean had risen just enough to cushion Spillane from fatality. The point is, despite all their training, neither Smith nor Spillane had any way of knowing when—or even whether—to jump. It turned out the pilot and the flight engineer, both of whom stayed on board until after the helicopter entered the water, survived with minimal injuries.

Seeing this show struck Will profoundly. Here were these almost impossibly high-skilled rescue workers faced with a situation in which they had no way of knowing what to do, yet needed to do *something*. It finally hit home: Will was going to have to act, to make a choice about his marriage, in the absence of certain knowledge and without any guarantee of the outcome.

Making decisions in the face of uncertainty is part of life. Usually the stakes are more on the order of: *If I go the back way, will I get there sooner? If I return his call today, will I look too eager? If I get the healthier granola bars, will the kids still eat them?*

But some walks of life entail habitual uncertainty coupled with potentially grave consequences. Firefighters, surgeons, triage nurses, hostage negotiators, miners, loggers, police officers, and soldiers all regularly face situations in which they have to take action based on imperfect knowledge—and where the repercussions of those actions might mean the difference between life and death. These are people who have to deal with the discomfort of acknowledging, "I don't know," and then get on with it.

Theorists have been contemplating how people make decisions when faced with uncertain knowledge at least since the seventeenth century, when the French mathematician and philosopher

Blaise Pascal wrote his *Pensées*, in which he set forth his famous wager. Using that ne plus ultra of unknowables—whether or not God exists—he argues that we cannot use reason to find the answer:

> If there is a God, He is infinitely incomprehensible, since, having neither parts nor limits, He has no affinity to us. We are then incapable of knowing either what He is or if He is.

We can't know for sure whether or not God exists, but Pascal concludes it's better to assume He does: "If you gain, you gain all; if you lose, you lose nothing." What interests me about Pascal's Wager is that it underscores how long humans have been preoccupied with the problem of not knowing, not merely as a threat to social standing, but as an existential dilemma. It shows how the prospect of being caught not knowing has ramifications beyond being dissed by your peers; it might just wreck your whole afterlife.

So how should we make decisions when we can't know what's right?

I don't know

"When Should I Trust My Gut?" a 2012 article in the journal *Organizational Behavior and Human Decision Processes*, suggests that intuition can be an effective substitute for knowledge. It outlines two studies, one in which participants rated the difficulty of basketball shots, another in which they were asked to judge whether designer pocketbooks were real or knockoffs. (Would it shock you to hear all three researchers were men? Can't you just picture them sitting around, coming up with the basketball idea, then going, "Wait—should we make this more gender balanced?" "Oh yeah, good idea. What's something women are good at?") At any rate, in both studies, half the group was asked to approach the task slowly and analytically, while the other half was asked to make quick, intuitive judgments. Those who were well-versed in the subject area—hoops or handbags, respectively—scored better when relying on pure intuition.

Science is nothing, though, if not a bastion of contradiction. Christopher Chabris and Daniel Simons, psychologists and authors of *The Invisible Gorilla: How Our Intuitions Deceive Us*, suggest relying on one's gut can be dangerous. Their book argues that intuitive beliefs are often mistaken ones, and that intuition's rise in popularity is faddish and foolhardy. "It has become fashionable to argue that intuitive methods of thinking and making decisions are superior to analytical methods," they write. "It is surprising how often we really have no clue."

That our intuition could lead us astray is troubling in direct proportion to the degree of trust we place in it. The solution would seem to be: Don't be overly trusting. Mix in a healthy dose of skepticism. But suppose we don't have a say in the matter? Suppose we're hardwired to trust—to believe in—our instincts, regardless of whether they're right? Suddenly the problem of not knowing becomes a lot more complicated.

The neurologist Robert A. Burton addresses this theory in his book *On Being Certain: Believing You Are Right Even When You're Not*. He suggests there are biological underpinnings that cause us to gravitate toward what he calls the feeling of knowing. Even when we try to be objective. Even when we're directly confronted with facts that contradict what we feel. He gives the example of hearing about the sudden death of a close friend:

Such upsetting news often takes time to "sink in." This disbelief associated with hearing about a death is an example of the sometimes complete disassociation between intellectual and felt knowledge.

Burton describes how the neural networks that link a thought to this feeling of knowing can be hard to undo, so that sometimes "an idea known to be wrong continues to feel correct." And he speculates about genetic variations that might make some of us hanker after certainty more than others. Scientists have already identified an inverse relationship between a specific gene (the DRD4 receptor gene) and the tendency to take risks; lower levels of this gene may be found, for example, in gambling addicts. Burton suggests we might similarly find evidence of a gene that links reward systems in the brain to an increased desire for the feeling of certainty. "Might the know-it-all personality trait," Burton wonders, "be seen as an addiction to the pleasure of the *feeling of knowing?*"

Even if it is in our nature, or our synapses, or our DNA, to enjoy feeling certain, that doesn't mean we have to give in to it—or that we should. It simply means we have to work that much harder to embrace doubt. As far back as Ancient Greece we find the idea that real wisdom begins with training an honest eye on one's limitations: on what we *don't* know. In Plato's *Apology*, Socrates describes a politician full of certainty, a man who "appeared to be wise in the opinion of most other men, and especially in his own opinion." Socrates then reasons that he himself must be wiser than this bigwig, for the simple reason that "I do not fancy I know what I do not know." In this formulation, what constitutes wisdom is at least in part our ability to be clear-sighted about our ignorance.

This gets echoed more than a millennium later in *The Divine Comedy*, when Saint Thomas Aquinas cautions Dante that "affection for one's own opinion binds, confines the mind." And again, many centuries after that, when the British literary critic William Empson said of Aristotle and Copernicus that they were "more intelligent (less at the mercy of their own notions)" than had been supposed. More recently Christopher Ricks revived this excellent locution in the *New York Times Book Review*, in whose pages he faulted the poet Robert Creeley for being "at the mercy of his own notions."

What does this have to do with saying "I don't know"? Simply that, in addition to strengthening our integrity and the authenticity of our connections with others, feeling free to say "I don't know" also allows us greater receptivity—which may lead to greater wisdom.

But this is harder than it sounds. We are all at the mercy of our notions, and the extent to which we forget this is the extent to which it imprisons us.

If making a searching inventory of our biases and striving for objectivity regarding our deepest beliefs contribute to sound decisions, it's little wonder that the history of decision theory has tended to favor analysis over intuition. The literature is crammed with classical decision-making models, each with a name more fabulously clunky and multisyllabic than the next, from the Rational-Economic Model to Bayesian Decision Analysis to Signal Detection Theory to Organizational Decision Making to Expected Utility Theory to (my favorite) Multi-Attribute Utility Analysis to (my other favorite) the Heuristic-Systematic Persuasion Model. But here's the thing: Most of the research that led to these paradigms looked at decision making in structured, controlled settings.

Then in 1988, something happened that led to a change in the way researchers understand how we make decisions under duress. A U.S. Naval warship in the Persian Gulf shot down an Iranian passenger plane, having incorrectly identified it as a hostile attacker. All 290 people on board, including 66 children, were killed. Although the United States government issued notes of regret for the loss of innocent life, it never admitted any wrongdoing. (Indeed, in a move that might have added a few pleats to the brow of William Empson, then Vice President George H. W. Bush said, "I'll never apologize for the United States of America. Ever. I don't care what the facts are.") Despite the government's outward stance of surety, that incident led the military to direct new energy toward understanding how people make tough decisions under difficult, high-stakes conditions. In 1989, the Army Research Institute convened the first naturalistic decision making (NDM) conference to do

just that. NDM looks at the decision-making prac-
tices not only of soldiers but also of firefighters,
critical care nurses, jurors, nuclear power plant
operators, anesthesiologists, meteorologists, high-
way engineers, even tournament chess players—all
kinds of real-life high-stress decision makers. And
what researchers have found is that these people,
working under extreme time pressure and in un-
predictable, rapidly fluctuating situations, did best
not by following the classical models (generating
and comparing sets of options) but by relying
on . . . drumroll, please . . . intuition.*

We seem to have come full circle, no? And via
the strangest route: Doesn't the military seem like
the least likely entity to advocate trusting your feelings? (*Just fire when you feel the vibe, man.*) Actually, when the military talks about intuition, it isn't
talking about mystical hunches. Gary Klein, a pio-
neer and leader in the field of NDM, defines intuition as a pattern-matching process, a means by
which we use previous experiences to categorize
and interpret unfolding events. Because emergen-

---

* Somewhat, er, *counterintuitively*, the military has fully embraced
both concept and parlance: The Army Field Manual on command
and control now includes a section on "intuitive decision making."

cies tend to unfold with lightning intensity, we don't take stock of this mental process and may wind up feeling our knowledge of how to act came through something inexplicable and occult, like extrasensory perception. In fact, ESP is what led to a breakthrough in Klein's research—or rather, not ESP itself, but a conversation with a fire commander who claimed to have ESP. Klein asked what made him think so.

The commander launched into a story about a time when a "sixth sense" had enabled him to save the lives of himself and his crew. He'd led his hose team into the living room of a house so they could aim their jets of water at what appeared to be a kitchen fire in the next room. Suddenly, the commander got an uneasy feeling and ordered his crew outside. No sooner had they reached the street than the living room floor caved in. Had the firefighters still been there, they'd have plummeted into the inferno that turned out to be raging in the basement. The commander insisted some kind of ESP had caused him to act.

But the more Klein probed, the more it emerged that several details about the incident didn't match the commander's expectations of a small, contained kitchen fire. (The temperature was too hot for the size of the blaze; the sound of the flames was strangely quiet; the flames engulfing the kitchen were unusually resistant to the hoses.) It turned out he'd been receiving all sorts of concrete clues, processing them subconsciously and at great speed, and then acting on them—without ever articulating or even being aware of his thought process.

This story shows how knowledge we're not even conscious of registering can influence us for the good. To paraphrase Empson, we might say of the fire commander that he was not so much at the mercy of his notions as held in their grace. But the opposite is an ever-present danger: Our unconsidered notions can have an ill effect, and the more reflexively we latch on to them, the more damage they might cause.

Consider the phenomenon of false confessions, which usually occur when two kinds of false knowledge coincide. The first is the false knowledge of law enforcement officials. In their book *Mistakes Were Made (but not by me): Why We Justify Fool-*

ish Beliefs, Bad Decisions, and Hurtful Acts, the social psychologists Carol Tavris and Elliot Aronson write:

> Currently, the professional training of most police officers, detectives, judges, and attorneys includes almost no information about their own cognitive biases; how to correct for them, as much as possible; and how to manage the dissonance they will feel when their beliefs meet disconfirming evidence.

Once interrogators believe they are questioning a guilty person, they are so programmed to get a confession that they may resort to extreme tactics. Tavris and Aronson cite a 2004 *New York Times* article about a brutal double homicide in which a detective admitted to lying in order to extract a confession. The suspect was the seventeen-year-old son of the murdered couple. The lie the detective told was that the father had emerged briefly from his coma before dying and told police his son was the attacker. "Under duress, suggestive questioning, and badgering," wrote the *Times*, the suspect "wondered aloud if he was deluded or had a dual personality and could have committed the killings and blocked the memory." He confessed to the crime and spent seventeen years in prison before the convictions were overturned.

The detective's justification for lying to the suspect? Confidence in what he "knew" to be true. "I don't think he did it," he told the *Times*. "I know he did it." Such swaggering certitude is hardly anomalous; training techniques systematically encourage it, while simultaneously reassuring interrogators that innocent people don't confess to crimes.

Except they do. This is the second, far more baffling, false knowledge that enables false confessions: the certainty of the accused that she has committed a crime when in fact she has not. Thanks to DNA testing and organizations like the Innocence Project, we finally have conclusive evidence that innocent people do make false confessions. Why on earth would anyone do this? It remains so hard to fathom that many people still cannot erase the belief that the convicted must be guilty.

A half century ago, the psychologist Melvin Lerner introduced his Belief in a Just World hypothesis, which holds that some people blame innocent victims as a way of protecting our belief

that the world is a fair and safe place. The fact
that the idea of false confessions still beggars our
belief—how many of us can wrap our minds
around confessing to something we didn't do?—is
testimony not only to the insidious power of interrogation techniques but also to the doggedness
of our own arrogant certainty that we would be able
to withstand them. Our certainty that we know
what we know.

Of course, sometimes a suspect tenders a false
confession knowingly, as a way to stop the anguish
of interrogation. But sometimes she actually buys
into the idea that she must have committed the
crime. How could a person become so disoriented
about her own self-knowledge? According to Ian
Herbert, writing in the Association for Psychologi-
cal Science journal the *Observer*, "The longer police
interrogate a suspect, emphatic about his guilt and
peppering their interrogation with details of the
crime, the more likely a suspect is to become con-
vinced himself."

Elizabeth Loftus is a psychologist whose research on the malleability of human memory has
gained worldwide attention. In one famous study,
she planted false memories, leading subjects erro-

neously to believe they had once, as children, become lost in a shopping mall. Subsequently, 25 percent of those subjects not only reported being able to remember the event but also supplied vivid details of the "memory."

In other words, they effectively *knew* the made-up event to have occurred.

"That's the frightening part," Loftus has said, "the truly horrifying idea that what we think we know, what we believe with all our hearts, is not necessarily the truth."

This is indeed a whole other level of saying "I don't know." It's scary to think that our own sense of what we know could be so pliable, so unreliable, so flimsy and fragile a thing. Surrendering a sense of control makes us feel vulnerable. But surrendering the illusion of control can also bring great peace—as well as possibility.

Three

In the course of researching this book I asked scores of people, friends and strangers, if they could think of a time when they'd covered up their ignorance or felt pressure to refrain from saying "I don't know." Some responded instantly with detailed anecdotes, painful, funny, or both. Some offered more general associations they had with the feeling of being caught not knowing. Others mused about the underlying reasons they had felt, at various times in their lives and with various audiences, more or less secure about exposing what they didn't know.

One person said, "No."

"No?"

"No. I've never felt that."

"Wow."

"I believe telling the truth should never be an act of courage."

"Oh." My mind went all swimmy. "You mean," I said, faltering, "telling the truth should be so much a *given* that doing so should never require an unusual feat of courage?"

"Yes."

I was flooded with a rush of muddled admiration—muddled because it was tinged with the regrettable knowledge that I was not in her league. While I don't think of myself as particularly craven or morally lax, for me telling the truth sometimes *does* require a special act of courage, not to say deliberate effort, a mustering of willpower, and occasionally even a period of private rehearsal.

But even as I marveled at her meritorious claim, I had a prickling, something's-not-quite-right-about-this-picture feeling.

My interviewee was indisputably a force: an international consultant, extremely self-possessed and well-informed, with a keen intelligence and a vocal cadence that suggested a habit of evaluating every word—swiftly, proficiently—before it left her mouth. As a diplomat's daughter, she'd had an upbringing unusually rich in travel, opportunity, exposure to ideas and experience, and access to information and power. She was poised, even polished, yet also palpably sympathetic and appealing. And I did not doubt her assertion; beyond all her other formidable attributes, she projected a profound sense of integrity.

So why my skepticism?

I thought of my partner, Mike, at that very moment with his kindergarten students, most of whom are children of color who qualify for free lunch, many whose first language is not English and whom the state classifies as "high needs." I replayed the consultant's maxim in my mind: *Telling the truth should never be an act of courage.* And thought of those little cherubs, those urchins, tearing around the playground or gathering on the rug; thought of their openness and their guardedness; thought of Mike pointing to the jumbled alphabet, saying, "Do you know what this letter is?" and of them composing their faces into masks, already at age four or five having learned how to be carefully inscrutable, and nodding: *yes.* And thought once more of the consultant, with her exceptional childhood and all its attendant advantages, not least of which was the fact that she had "always been encouraged to ask lots of questions."

Telling the truth requires no special courage *so long as the cost is nil*. But the ability to say "I don't know" derives in no small part from privilege.

When my brother, Andy, got his first job after earning a master's degree in public policy, he was startled to receive clear messages that the primary reason he'd been hired was his color. I am white; my brother, black. I am the biological daughter and he the adopted son of our white parents.

This was the midnineties. Andy was hired as a research analyst for a nationally renowned company that conducts evaluations of programs such as Head Start, Medicaid, and WIC, the federal food and nutrition program for low-income women and children. His first day on the job, he was sitting in his new office when an e-mail to all staff appeared in his in-box. He suspects it wasn't really meant for his eyes. It stated that the active recruitment effort for "minority hires" had concluded, the need having been met. It turned out that the woman who'd previously occupied his office was African-American. Andy was the only black professional on staff.

As a research analyst, Andy would make periodic site visits, flying with a coworker to one of the cities involved in an ongoing study. They'd stay in a motel for four or five days and spend their time interviewing both administrators of the program in question and consumers of that program's services. Andy regularly got sent to the sites with the highest levels of poverty and violence—Watts, Memphis, Detroit. He remembers the fear and discomfort his white coworkers displayed when they visited particularly rough neighborhoods. Once, as Andy steered the rental car down a street lined by burned-out buildings alternating with storefront churches, liquor stores, and check-cashing places, an African-American man stepped off the curb, waiting for their car to go by so he could cross. Andy remembers his white colleague recoiling in the passenger seat and shrieking, "Please don't hurt me!" Another time, interviewing a woman who lived in Section 8 housing, Andy noticed his coworker was visibly ill at ease in the dark, fusty

apartment. At the interview's conclusion, she scur-
ried down the broken sidewalk to their car, locked
the door quickly behind her, and exclaimed with
revulsion, "How could someone *live* like that?"

The site visits, which generated the raw data,
were considered entry-level work. After a year on
the job, Andy asked his supervisor if he could
take on some more challenging assignments—
participating in some of the data analysis that con-
stituted the meat of the reports—and was flatly
turned down. "We need you on those site visits,"
he was told. He was a "good escort in the 'hood."

Increasingly conscious of being valued as a
quota-filler and a glorified bodyguard, Andy gave
enormous care to his writing when submitting reports of his site visits. In one instance, he sent
a report to the senior researcher with a note explaining it was "a seasoned draft," a reference to its
being the most recent iteration of a paper that had
already been through a series of revisions. The senior researcher, perhaps acting out of his own discomfort at being unfamiliar with the phrase, openly
mocked him. "'Seasoned'?" He gave a short laugh.
"What, did you use salt and pepper?"

"I felt like it was a risk for me to say anything,"

Andy reflects. "I constantly had to go that extra step to prove legitimacy. And the atmosphere made me absolutely less inclined to ask for help. If I made a mistake, it would be magnified. If I admitted not knowing something, I'd be judged as being less than what I'm capable of."

This was at a company whose lengthy diversity statement reads, in part:

> Here, diversity translates into an inclusive work environment, where differences in experience, ethnic backgrounds, cultures, and lifestyles add strength and value to our core mission—providing the social policy community with objective, high-quality information collection and analysis . . . [Our] ongoing commitment to diversity is also woven into everyday actions, policies, and practices. We are committed to maintaining a work environment in which everyone is treated with respect and dignity.

I doubt anyone at the company sought to create an environment that would have a chilling effect on my brother's ability to say "I don't know."

In fact, given the company's ethos and the kinds of programs it focused its research on, I suspect his colleagues would be horrified to hear they'd contributed to such an environment. (Do you see where I'm going with this?) Chances are, they never thought about it. They acted out of limited understanding, out of ignorance. Chances are, they *just didn't know*.

Whether intended or not, the effects of such an environment can be so galling and undermining as to stymie growth and impede the very goals the institution espouses. Valerie is a professor emerita of art at a small New England college. Her own work in photography has been widely praised and exhibited. Yet as a woman working in the latter part of the twentieth century, she frequently faced gender bias from both colleagues and students, manifested in the courses she was given to teach (often introductory level) and in the students' unconcealed preference for male professors (automatically assumed to be the more technically knowledgeable in a field like photography).

In the early nineties, after Valerie had been teaching for over a quarter of a century, her college dismantled its darkrooms to make room for computers. Simultaneously, she was saddled with teaching a new course: digital photography. Digital cameras were just coming on the market, and Valerie found herself completely out of her element. For decades, she'd comported herself gracefully under the burden of others' baseless condescension. Now, in a bitter irony, she found her skills *matching* people's low expectations. Her expertise, built up with so much time and care, lay in the arenas of darkroom skills, artistic expression, and the meanings of images. Suddenly these counted for nothing. Students were marching up to her with their shiny new high-tech devices, all different models with different sets of operating instructions, expecting her to tell them how each and every one worked. "I was miserable and depressed," she recalls. "They knew that I didn't know."

After having long prided herself on running an egalitarian classroom, she saw she could no longer afford to; she felt authority slipping from her as the technology in her field leapt ahead. Eventually, against her deepest sense of who she was and what she believed in, she found herself "throwing it back on them a little," using the culture of shame and hierarchy to put her students on the defensive.

She became adept at saying, with a disparaging little sniff, "I'm sorry. If you don't bring in your manual, I can't help." The learning environment had become a face-saving environment, benefiting no one.

In time, Valerie gained the knowledge she needed to teach again with confidence. But looking back now on those interim efforts to hide her ignorance, she says, "It's almost too painful to remember. I had learned to be a little bit mean."

Refraining from saying "I don't know" when we are conscious of making that choice is one thing, but what about all those times we don't *know* we don't know? Arguably a more pernicious problem, not least because it is by definition so much harder to identify. One arena in which it's frequently played out is education—particularly when teachers do not share the culture of their students.

Lisa Delpit, an educator, author, and MacArthur Fellow, has criticized Teach For America—which sends predominantly white recruits into schools that are concentrated overwhelmingly in poor communities of color—not because of the cultural difference per se, but because of the lack of adequate preparation that would help orient these fledgling teachers to think about the implications of cultural difference. She has asked groups of young people about to embark on their first teaching experience, "How would you prepare yourselves if you learned you were going to be teaching in Kenya next September?"

The ready reply: "We'd learn about the culture."

"How?"

Eagerly: "We'd study the idioms, music, history, literature, geography, food, politics, gender roles, religious beliefs, folk tales, family structure, dress . . ."

"And what," she asks, "have you been doing to prepare yourselves to teach the students you'll be working with next September in this country?"

The silence this question invariably meets hangs swollen with epiphany.

In an interview with *Education Week*, Delpit has said:

> I want black children to have the opportunity
> to have teachers who understand their culture,

their intellectual legacy, their communities, the best ways to teach them, the best ways to motivate them, the best ways to connect to their parents, etc. Those people can be of any color. It is not the color that matters as much as the connections. While many black teachers have an easier time connecting, I have seen black teachers who cannot con-nect with certain black children because their backgrounds were so different. I have seen many white teachers who can connect be-cause they have been humble enough to know that they have to learn a great deal about their students to be good teachers.

Some people embrace the idea that the solution to racism is willed blindness. If we "overlook" dif-ferences, the problems will go away. This is a lot like treating ignorance with ignorance: What I don't know about you won't hurt, so long as we both pretend not to notice the gap. This practice might work out pretty well for those with power, less so for the disenfranchised—and for anyone interested in increasing the opportunities for and caliber of connections between people. When we strive for "color blindness," we foreclose not only on the examination of our own unconscious biases, but also on the possibility of knowing others in all their nuanced complexity.

Christine Sleeter, an education reformer and antiracism activist, describes in an interview with *Rethinking Schools* magazine why this may be particularly problematic in the classroom:

> In a color-blind approach, there is a whole lot about a student that you are not seeing. For example, if you take a kid who is of Mexican descent and you say, "I don't see a Mexican kid, I just see a kid," you are preventing yourself from knowing something about that student's culture and community—and an important part of the student.

To *prevent yourself from knowing something* about your students—doesn't quite have the ring of sound pedagogy, does it? Even if one subscribes to the most rigid, traditional model of education, perceiving it as nothing more than the transmission of knowledge from teacher to student (much like the baton handoff in a relay race), it nevertheless follows that the transaction is most likely to succeed (the baton most likely to fit snugly into the palm of the receiving runner) if the teacher is able to *see* the student she's handing off to.

The ignorance we're ignorant of is the ignorance most difficult to remedy.

On a freezing January afternoon in 1982, a Florida-bound Boeing 737 sat on the runway at Washington National Airport. Earlier in the day, the airport had been closed due to heavy snow. Now, although the storm had slackened, flakes continued to fall. Sitting in the cockpit, waiting to be cleared for takeoff, the copilot engaged the captain in conversation about the weather.

> **Copilot**: *(Talking about another aircraft visible through the windshield.)* Look how the ice is just hanging on his, ah, back, back there, see that?
>
> **Captain**: . . .
>
> **Copilot**: See all those icicles on the back there and everything?
>
> **Captain**: Yeah.

I don't know

A little later, the copilot referred to the long period of time that had elapsed since their own wings had been deiced:

Copilot: Boy, this is a, this is a losing battle here on trying to deice those things, it [gives] you a false feeling of security, that's all it does.

He brought up the topic of the weather again after they received clearance:

Copilot: Let's check these tops again since we been setting here awhile.
Captain: I think we get to go here in a minute.

And once more, looking at the instrument readings just before takeoff:

Copilot: That don't seem right, does it? Ah, that's not right.
Captain: Yes it is, there's eighty.
Copilot: Naw, I don't think that's right. Ah, maybe it is.
Captain: Hundred and twenty.
Copilot: I don't know.

Then, its wings crusted with snow and ice, the plane sped down the runway. It got off the ground, but would not properly climb. It remained airborne for thirty-seven seconds before crashing into the 14th Street Bridge, where it sheared the tops off cars and plunged into the ice-clogged Potomac. All but five of the seventy-nine people on board died, along with four motorists. Upon analyzing the black box recorder found in the submerged wreckage, the National Transportation Safety Board determined the probable cause of the crash to be pilot error: specifically, a failure of communication within the cockpit. The copilot had been trying to warn the captain. The captain apparently did not know it.

Or wasn't able to hear it. Or, not wanting to return to the gate for deicing after having waited in a taxi line for close to an hour before reaching the runway, chose not to realize it. Interestingly, the NTSB's official accident report said that while the captain had "good operational skills and knowledge," he had twice failed a line check—once for receiving unsatisfactory grades in "adherence to regulations, checklist usage, [and] flight procedures," and another time for deficiencies in knowledge of aircraft limitations. The same report described the copilot as a "witty, sharp individual," and reported that people who'd flown with him during stressful operations (he had been a fighter pilot in the Air Force) referred to him as someone "who knew his limitations."

The ability to know one's limitations, to recognize the bounds of one's own comprehension—this is a kind of knowing that approaches wisdom. But are there circumstances in which our own psyches flout us, stand in the way of our abilities to discern what we know from what we don't?

My friend Jane was nine when her family moved into a new suburban development in Southern California. Three houses down lived an older, childless couple, Mr. and Mrs. W, who seemed to Jane wonderfully bookish and cultured. Mr. W wore three-piece suits, played the violin, and spent hours in his study, researching and writing books about classical music. Jane began to spend afternoons at the Ws' house, helping Mr. W organize his notes, thrilled by his promise to mention her name in his next book. The Ws were like highly cultured substitute grandparents. They took her out to elegant restaurants, even brought her on weekend trips to Mexico. Jane's younger sister, Karen, wheedled to go along, but their parents told her she was too young. "These are Jane's special friends," they explained, amused and perhaps flattered that their daughter had been singled out for such special attentions from this refined, dignified couple. This was the late sixties.

One day Mr. W showed Jane a roomful of pornography, all of it meticulously indexed and organized. He began inviting her to sit in the master bedroom while he shaved in the adjoining bathroom. He began to touch her, just a little. He began, when they went away together for the weekend, to rise during the night from the bed he shared with his wife and slip into Jane's bed. Through it all, striving to be seen as good, as mannerly, as refined and worthy of the attentions of this estimable figure, she kept her silence. Then one day Mr. W removed his belt, saying he had something special to show Jane, and all at once she regained custody of her tongue. "No," she said. "No. No." And got up and walked straight out the front door and didn't stop until she reached home.

She never told her family the reason she

stopped visiting the Ws. "I made up something about being too old." Her parents seemed incurious; her younger sister saw opportunity.

Karen was six when she began spending afternoons at the Ws. Jane remembers a day, bright with sunshine, when Karen stood in the kitchen, poised to go out, her hand on the knob, the door ajar, the knob glinting gold in the sun. "Where are you going?" asked Jane. "The Ws," Karen replied, and paused. She seemed to wait. For a queer, protracted moment, the sisters looked into each other's eyes. "Okay, then," said Jane, as if from a fog. "See you later."

Karen, as her sister had done before her, began spending nearly every afternoon at the Ws', as well as some evenings, and also going away with them on weekends. After a year of this there came a day when she fell suddenly and strangely ill. Their mother in a panic called the doctor, who rushed to the house, laid the seven-year-old down on the bathroom floor, and pumped her stomach. She had swallowed the entire contents of a bottle of baby aspirin. All the little pink chewable pills came up out of her body.

Their mother turned to Jane, who stood watching from the doorway. "Do you know anything about this?"

"No," Jane heard herself say. Slowly shaking her head: "I don't know."

In adulthood, Karen came across Mr. W's obituary in the local paper. This led to her telling Jane about the abuse, which was horrific; it included being raped by Mr. W while his wife watched, and being filmed by Mr. W while other men raped her. Mr. W said if she told anyone he'd kill her dog, describing in detail the way he would do it.

These revelations released in Jane her own locked-away memories. Together the sisters told their parents the story, but gently, tempering it, not wanting to inflict unbearable guilt. Even so, their parents were sickened and distraught. How could they have failed to know or suspect? Neither Jane nor Karen ever blamed them. "The Ws were so outwardly respectable," Jane says. "It was a much more innocent time. There was nothing about sexual abuse on TV or in the movies, in books or in school." The first federal legislation addressing the issue, the Child Abuse Prevention and Treatment Act, would not be enacted until 1974, seven years after Karen's ordeal. "And," adds Jane, "children can be very good secret keepers."

For a long time Jane felt her own guilt might tear her apart. She still thinks often of that single moment, a year before her sister's suicide attempt, when Karen paused with her hand on the bright doorknob, as if waiting for Jane to speak. How Jane wishes she had said, "Don't go!"

But for all her regrets and all her sorrow, Jane understands that in that moment she had been incapable of rescuing her sister. Incapable because she had been cut off not simply from speech but from knowledge. "My brain," she says, "had already decided not to know."

Repressed knowledge is the flip side of the false knowledge discussed in the last chapter: the innocents who "know" they committed crimes, the study subjects who "know" they got lost in the mall. Together, these represent the most chilling kinds of not knowing: the ignorance which is beyond not simply our control but also our ability to realize—at least without a healing epiphany or therapeutic care. Chilling, but not hopeless. The more we talk about the limits of knowledge and the dangers of false knowledge, the more we create a landscape in which true knowledge may be discerned.

And these landscapes are as badly needed in large arenas as in small. For just as one psyche may wall off painful knowledge as a defense against what the individual finds intolerable, whole institutions may engage in similar behavior on a broad scale: Witness the Catholic Church, still reeling from a clergy sex abuse scandal that spans decades and continents. Although the original crimes are sexual in nature, the more grievous crime might be that of institutional-level willed ignorance, judging from the fact that most of the public outrage has focused not on the individuals who committed the assaults but on the Church's efforts to cloak itself in a shroud of not knowing.

Is there a wrong way to say "I don't know"? Yes. When we declare ignorance, it should be a) honest and b) in the spirit of opening ourselves up to hearing, to learning, to receiving. When we say "I don't know" under these conditions, the words can forge connection, healing, growth. But when we resist or disavow knowledge, when we profess ignorance as a way of donning armor and evading accountability, then we make a mockery of those words, and we rupture connections not only with others but within ourselves, within our souls.

Of course the flagrant refusal to know is hardly limited to situations involving sexual abuse. Perhaps the most infamous example of a nation adopting a posture of not knowing is World War II–era Germany, where official state policies facilitated Holocaust denial in a multitude of ways, even as the genocide was unfolding. Heinrich Himmler, in a speech to SS generals, declared the mass murder of Jews a secret, never to be recorded; Nazis destroyed evidence of mass graves at many killing centers; Hitler ordered the use of euphemisms such as "action" for violent operations and "special treatment" for killing. And of course there is the infamous story of Theresienstadt, the ghetto/labor camp that in June 1944 was temporarily spruced up in order to show representatives from the International Red Cross how well the Nazis treated the Jews. In his novel *Austerlitz*, W. G. Sebald describes the hoax:

> [The representatives] could see for themselves the friendly, happy folk who had been spared the horrors of war and were looking out of the

windows, could see how smartly they were all dressed, how well the few sick people were cared for, how they were given proper meals served on plates, how the bread ration was handed out by people in white drill gloves, how posters advertising sporting events, cabarets, theatrical performances, and concerts were being put on every corner and how, when the day's work was over, the residents of the town flocked out in their thousands on the ramparts and bastions to take the air, almost as if they were passengers enjoying an evening stroll on the deck of an oceangoing steamer, a most reassuring spectacle, all things considered, which the Germans [filmed], whether for propaganda purposes or in order to justify their actions and conduct to themselves.

Such an elaborate sham. All that energy, expended not simply to prevent the world at large from knowing the truth but perhaps also, as Sebald suggests, as a way the Nazis tried to manage their own psychic dilemma: that is, a way of simultaneously knowing and not knowing the atrocities they were committing.

Another example of state-sponsored not-knowing and erasing—although not nearly at the same proportions or with the same motivations as Nazi Germany—may be found in present-day Israel. Yishai, a lawyer and law professor who grew up in Israel, served as a paratrooper in the Israeli Defense Forces in the nineties. Although military service is obligatory, Yishai joined with a real sense of enthusiasm, a belief in the honor and nobility of serving that easily trumped any concerns about the political reality in Israel and Palestine and what role he might play in the conflict as a soldier. "As a young Israeli," he says, "a certain narrative is constructed for you: what it means to a Jew, an Israeli." This narrative hinges largely on the Holocaust and the idea that ensuring the viability and safety of the Jewish state is a moral imperative, necessary to prevent such an atrocity from ever happening again. Yishai recounts the plethora of ways the Holocaust gets intertwined with the existence of the Jewish state, not least by the services and celebrations that mark Yom HaShoah, or Holocaust Remembrance Day, and Yom Ha'atzmaut, or Independence Day, which fall close together on the calendar. From the time children are small, an inextricable link is made between the two, in schools as well as in media, which display graphic images of wide-eyed toddlers wearing Stars of David, crates of confiscated wedding rings, emaciated prisoners marching at gunpoint, and heaps and heaps of naked bodies.

"Of course, there is reality in that narrative," says Yishai, whose grandmother is a survivor, and who has many other family members who were killed in the Holocaust. "But it also gets used in the service of a nationalistic agenda to justify actions that in my view—based on my sense of myself as a human being and as a Jew—are morally wrong." The irony is that the same nation that has dedicated so much energy to refusing to forget—committed itself to bearing eternal witness so that what happened may never happen again—that same nation cultivates a different kind of not knowing.

As a teenager on hikes with his friends in the mountains surrounding Jerusalem, Yishai remembers being touched with something like melancholy wonder whenever they'd come across an old olive grove or a cluster of prickly pears—likely signs that a Palestinian village had once thrived in that spot. Some 250 Palestinian villages were erased in the vicinity of Jerusalem when the modern state of Israel was established. But if ever Yishai said, "You know, people *lived* here not so long ago," his friends mocked him for his sentimentality. It was a silly thing, something you weren't supposed to notice or, if you did notice, care about. "The olive trees became a running joke with my friends. I don't think it is a coincidence that Jewish settlers target olives trees for mutilation in the West Bank and that Jerusalem's surroundings were forested with European pine trees soon after 1967—the olive trees, some of which are hundreds of years old, are a reminder, a memory of a people in a place.

"I think there's a deliberate effort to keep young people from knowing or thinking about these issues in this way," says Yishai. "On a national level, you want to forget that there are fellow human beings who paid a price—and continue to do so—for you having a homeland."

For him, the end of forgetting came at age nineteen. He was on duty with three other soldiers, patrolling the Jabaliya refugee camp in Gaza. It was 1992, a time of relative calm. As they walked through the poor Arab neighborhood, through the narrow alleyways, dressed in their uniforms and carrying their guns, they turned a corner only to surprise some children who'd been playing there, squatting in the alley: a pair of boys, perhaps two and four years old. The children looked up and immediately the color drained from their faces. Crying, screaming in abject terror, they fled on their small, panicked legs.

"Whatever idea I had of myself," says Yishai, "I was perceived by them as a monster." This relatively benign interaction—absent any violence save for the violence of the children's fright—shook him to his core. He did not discuss it with his comrades. "As a soldier," he says, "you're trained to forget parts of yourself." But from then on it became impossible to forget, impossible to disavow his awareness that his own humanity was linked to the humanity of the Palestinians in the camps he was ordered to patrol. And although he remained in the service for the full three years and went on to become a sergeant, from that moment forth he hated being a soldier, especially when it placed him in direct contact with Palestinian people.

How does one reconcile knowledge with the shutting off of knowledge? In Yishai's case, he finished his military service, grew out his hair, went backpacking in South America, and began a long process of recovery that involved studying modern Hebrew poetry, Arabic, and law, with the goal of becoming a human rights attorney who would represent Palestinians in the Israeli court system. He now specializes in mediation, a field that requires the ability to "contain different perspectives."

In the case of Frances Pratt, being told to suppress knowledge of injustice in childhood led to a lifetime's commitment to bringing such knowledge to light. Mrs. Pratt was born in 1935 in Chester County, South Carolina. "It was so rural," she says, "we lived plum nearly out of the state. It was so small, the train wouldn't stop. It'd just slow down so you could jump out into the sawdust pile." Then, just in case you didn't realize, she adds kindly, "That's my joke about it."

In 1947, when she was twelve years old, Frances and her mother took a bus to Raleigh, North Carolina. Her mother, a sharecropper who raised cotton and corn, had little time or money for travel, but Frances's older brother had sent them bus tickets so they could visit him in his new hometown. They went in high summer, in between planting and harvesting seasons. When they arrived in Raleigh, it was hot as blazes. They saw an ice cream parlor near the station. Frances's mother said, "I'm going to buy you an ice cream," and they stepped inside the shop.

"We don't serve niggers in here," called the clerk. ("That's the word he used," Mrs. Pratt explains when she tells the story today. "I'm telling it like it is.") "Y'all go around the side," he instructed. "I stick it through the window."

Frances was angry and afraid. "Let's not have any," she whispered.

Her mother repeated: "I'm going to buy you an ice cream."

They went around the side of the building. Frances's mother put her money through the window and the clerk stuck out two vanilla cones. "Don't tell your brother," her mother warned. "He'll come down here and start something and they'll put him in jail."

So Frances stood in the glaring heat of the yard, her cone melting in her hand, rocked by the suddenly urgent need to protect her brother from knowing what had happened; rocked, too, by a new kind of ache for her mother. Back in Chester County, she had never seen her mother treated in this detestable way. Fear made her keep her mouth shut, but she promised herself there under the punishing sun that when she grew bigger she would not keep quiet about what she knew, especially where injustice was concerned. And as a teenager she took a bus north (wearing an outfit supplied by the local undertaker), where she studied to become a nurse and eventually was elected president of the Nyack, New York, branch of the NAACP, a position she has held for over thirty years and in which she has made good on that childhood promise.

We can feel pressure to pretend we know. We can feel pressure to pretend we don't know. Either way, there are sometimes extremely compelling reasons for going along with the pretense. In the case of Mrs. Pratt, keeping silent about what she'd witnessed might have prevented her brother not just from being jailed but from being lynched.

At the other end of the spectrum, we find less dire, but no less caring, reasons to keep silent: to spare the feelings of another. Suppose a person you do not recall having laid eyes on strikes up a conversation in which it becomes clear you have previously met. Not only that, it emerges he remembers all sorts of things about you: your occupation, what kind of dog you have, how you like your eggs. At that point do you say, *Er . . . what was your name?* Miss Manners would have you do precisely that (actually, Miss Manners advises "total self-abasement"), but I myself have been known simply to smile and hold my tongue.

Or suppose your very own sweetheart comes up to you and says, with tender conviction: "You know that time when we took the gondola ride in the sunset and you said my eyes were like limpid pools?" Do you say, *No, dearest, I do not*, or do you squint in a fond, vague sort of way and say, *Mmm . . . I think so. When was that?* Sociolinguists call this, rather marvelously, dispreferred response avoidance. In other words, sometimes we avoid saying "I don't know" less from a desire to save face than from a desire to gratify the other party. To facilitate positive social intercourse. To be kind.

But pretense for the sake of courtesy has its dangers—regardless of whether it's knowledge or ignorance we're pretending to have. A friend shares a story about her long-ago marriage:

In the midst of the great sadness of my divorce, one of the most helpful things a counselor asked me was, "Are you stupid?" This may sound harsh, but it was asked matter-of-factly, not insultingly, and helped begin the long process of bringing me back to myself, into my own form of knowledge, out of the too-long-held posture of my ceding all "knowing" to my husband.

In an effort to accommodate her husband's need to occupy the role of "knower" in their relationship, she had effaced her own wisdom and intelligence to the point where she hardly knew herself anymore.

Anya Malcolm tells a story about just the opposite: that is, about refusing to cede her "knowing," even when it entailed resorting to a bold, risky decision. As a college freshman in the late eighties, at a large West Coast university, she enrolled in a philosophy seminar taught by a professor reputed to be brilliant but sexist. This didn't worry her until she got her first paper back—with a C minus. She knew it was a good paper, even an excellent paper, and soon discovered that while a few men in the class had gotten A's and B's, among the women the grades were uniformly lower. She went back to her dorm room and thought hard. Asking to meet with the professor and discuss the paper was out; by then she'd heard more stories confirming his categorical dismissal of women's cognitive abilities, and she'd experienced firsthand his undisguised contempt. The other female students seemed resigned to accept his version of who they were, at least within the arena of his classroom: to cower politely and play the feebleminded bimbos he thought they were.

Anya could not. Every fiber of her being railed against it: against submitting to his version of her, against becoming complicit in his pretense of "knowing" women are dumb. But no matter how hard she thought, she could see no way around the problem—nothing short of becoming a man. So, like a heroine in a Shakespeare comedy, that's what she did. She handed in her next paper under the name Adam Malcolm.

On the day their graded papers were due back, the professor plucked one from the pile and sang its praises at length, extolling it as one of the best essays an undergraduate had ever submitted, elaborating on its robust and original thesis, the supple lucidity of its argument, the elegant concision of its prose. At last he said, "Will Adam Malcolm please stand?"

Anya rose.

He turned to her with displeasure. "I didn't call on you."

"Yes," she told him. "You did."

Decades later, hearing this story, I feel a shiver of trepidation even as I thrill at her bravery. "Weren't you afraid?" I ask.

"No."

What did she feel, in that moment after revealing her identity, standing there, exposed and proud, having dared to *know* herself in all her intelligence and personhood?

"I felt," she says, "as though every ounce of oxygen in the room had made a quick exit. I felt frozen in time. I felt . . ." And here she pauses, and when she next speaks it is with quiet aplomb. "A wonderful sense of peace and composure."

Four

In David Lodge's 1975 novel *Changing Places*, a send-up of academic pomposities, characters play a parlor game called Humiliation in which players name classical works of literature they have not read. The winner is he who names the work least unread by others in the party, thereby achieving for himself the greatest purported degree of humiliation. Of course, the joke is that only the most highly literate would find the game amusing in the first place. The self-outings are mere tokens; the game is really an opportunity for some backhanded self-puffery.

The game Lodge invented has o'erflowed the borders of fiction and come to be embraced by real-life academics. One scholar I know tells of playing it with a bunch of colleagues on an Edinburgh-bound train from Dundee, where they'd all been attending a James Joyce convention. After several noisy rounds, a gentleman sitting a few rows away stood and rotated to address them over the back of his seat. "I have a doctorate in modern literature from Oxford," he pronounced majestically, "and I've never read a word of D. H. Lawrence." The entire train compartment erupted in hilarious applause and the competition ended there, the posh interloper its uncontested winner.

With its distinctive flavor of braggadocio masquerading as humility, the game proposes an intriguing thesis on the magnetism of shame: Perhaps in an effort to master our dread of it, we flirt with its toothless cousin, much as we might symbolically vanquish a hated tyrant by burning him in effigy.

But although the game might be played exclusively among academics, the dread is hardly limited to the ivory tower. How else to explain the thriving niche economy that preys upon this insecurity? Here's just a smattering of titles in the current crop of self-help books: *The Art of Faking It: Sounding Smart Without Really Knowing Anything*; *The Concise Guide to Sounding Smart at Parties: An Irreverent Compendium of Must-Know Info from Sputnik to Smallpox and Marie Curie to Mao*; *How to Impress Anybody: Sound Smarter Than You Are About Everything from Aerodynamics to Zen Buddhism*; *How to Talk About Books You Haven't Read*; *The Intellectual Devotional: Revive Your Mind, Complete Your Education, and Roam Confidently with the Cultured Class*; *An Incomplete Education: 3,684 Things You Should Have Learned but Probably Didn't*; *Everything You Pretend to Know and Are Afraid Someone Will Ask*.

And even if none of the above pertains—even if you already know all that stuff—rest assured there's likely still something to feel insecure about. Students at the Massachusetts Institute of Technology may be able to explain cold fusion and, I don't know, the proof for Fermat's Last Theorem, but do they know how to butter their bread? For the past twenty years, MIT has been running an annual tongue-in-cheek charm school that aims to rectify such deficits as uncertainty about whether to hold a wineglass by its stem or bowl, how to cut lettuce, and what to do with your napkin when you go to the bathroom. Graduates are awarded ChDs (doctors of charm).

How about a school that teaches people to say "I don't know"?

More and more, medical schools are assuming this responsibility. This is notable because it represents a major divergence from the culture of traditional Western medicine. "Doctors use information as part of the therapeutic regimen," wrote the philosopher Sissela Bok in 1978. "It is given out in amounts, in admixtures, and according to timing believed best for patients. Accuracy, by comparison, matters far less." She points out that Plato, in his *Republic*, says that because physicians may use falsehood as a form of healing, they enjoy a right to dissemble that laymen do not. And she suggests that doctors might at times feel, with reason, duty-bound to conceal what they do not know:

> Physicians know only too well how uncertain a diagnosis or prognosis can be. They know how hard it is to give meaningful and correct

answers regarding health and illness. They also know that disclosing their own uncertainty or fears can reduce those benefits that depend upon faith in recovery.

Hiding uncertainty has been ingrained as part of a physician's job, although medical students absorb this lesson not so much via straightforward instruction (*Now, class, you must at all times maintain an aura of knowing*) as through operant conditioning: receiving viscerally aversive stimulus when they acknowledge they don't know.* An oncologist recalls a fairly standard example of this. She was a third-year student on rounds when the resident told her to look at the computer screen where the patient's comprehensive metabolic panel—a sea of complicated letters and numbers—was displayed. "What does this value mean?" he asked, pointing at one of the figures.

"I don't know," she freely admitted.

---

* Medicine is hardly the only field in which shame is used to remind inferiors of their place in a hierarchy. A friend who worked as a quantitative methods specialist on Wall Street and holds a bachelor's degree from MIT tells how senior colleagues disparaged everything below doctoral level mathematics as "folk math."

"*What?*" His voice grew lower and more scathing with each successive word. "You. Don't. Know. *That?*"

She felt she should quit right then, felt she was an imposter, a fraud. Decades later as she retells the story, her cheeks burn red.

My friend Pam became a psychiatrist after a brief career as a social worker. "In medical school," she says, "there's this pressure to know it all. You stand around the patient and the attending asks a question. 'What is the differential diagnosis for this abdominal pain?' And you're just hoping you have the answer, the pearl. That's what they're called: knowledge pearls. It's completely different from the social sciences, where multiple perspectives are valued, where you write essays, where you discuss theory. In medical school there's one answer. That's the pearl."

Another doctor, an obstetrician, tells of a time when, as a new intern, she was asked by the attending physician to assist on a postpartum tubal ligation—a procedure she'd not witnessed before. Eagerly, she did. Two days later, the chief of obstetrics asked her to assist with the same procedure.

"You've done this?" the chief asked. "You know what you're doing?"

Yes, said the new intern with a concerted air of confidence.

The chief handed her the scalpel. "Go ahead."

Scrupulously, meticulously, the new intern cut into the woman's abdomen exactly as she had seen the first doctor do—and made an incision four times as long as the chief had told his patient her scar would be.

"I should have said, 'Show me how you want the incision done,'" the obstetrician now says. "I should have said, 'I've seen one of these, but I've never done it myself.' But I was so anxious to show him I knew what I was doing."

Later, the new intern and the chief went to visit the patient together as she lay in recovery, and the chief delivered a lesson that only reinforced the professional premium on concealing uncertainty. Rather than tell the patient the truth, he delivered a self-serving lie. "Circumstances were tough in your case," he said smoothly, "but we managed by making the incision a little longer."

The culture that produced these stories is

changing. Part of physicians' reluctance to reveal uncertainty or acknowledge mistakes stems from the very real fear of malpractice suits. In 1986, Massachusetts became the first state to forbid the use of a doctor's apology as evidence of wrongdoing. Today, thirty-five states and the District of Columbia have enacted similar "I'm sorry" laws. Studies indicate that these laws, and the concomitant rise in physician honesty, have led to reduced anger in patients as well as lower settlement costs when malpractice suits are brought.

But it's complicated. Sometimes patients are the ones pressing doctors to don the costume of all-knowing, all-powerful healer.

"One patient made me very nervous," says another obstetrician, "by putting me up on a Godlike pedestal. She'd say, 'I *know* you won't let anything happen to me or my baby.' I'd be very careful in how I'd reply. I'd say, 'I'll do the best I can.'"

It became a kind of dance, a nervous two-step they'd play out at every visit, with the patient, who'd had numerous pelvic surgeries and a hard time getting pregnant, not-so-subtly exhorting the doctor to promise what he could not possibly know for sure, and the doctor trying to walk a fine line between placation and honesty. "She really seemed to need me to know, for her own psychic well-being. Each time I stopped short of telling her I knew everything would be okay, I felt I was cutting her legs out from under her. Eventually I found myself not quite assenting, but not quite disabusing her, either." In the end, mother and baby were fine, but the doctor was left with a residue of discomfort.

Still, more and more health-care providers are becoming both sanguine and prolific with their "I don't knows."

"Are you kidding?" says Jessi, a midwife. "I tell patients I don't know all the time. I tell them I'm stumped. I'm just not willing to fake it. That would be so much worse for me. I'd rather have them think I'm stupid."

"My patients generally appreciated it when I'd say I didn't know," affirms a retired internist. "I'd say I'm going to do some research and get back to them. Or I'd step out into the hall and consult with a colleague who might have experience with this issue. I'd think, 'Who can I bring in who has gray hair?'"

Pam, my psychiatrist friend, talks about how

essential it is that she keep her sights on how little she can ever know. As a brand-new social worker, she was once conducting an intake interview when the client interrupted: "Can you just be quiet and listen to me?" Pam was taken aback, but complied, and soon realized the client had been correct; the intake questions didn't fit what the client needed to say.

Patients often tell Pam, "You have no idea what I'm going through." Although initially her impulse was to offer solace in the form of empathy, to reassure them that she *did* know, she has since learned to say, "You're absolutely right. Please tell me what it's like. I don't know, but I can listen."

"Most people go into this field because we have a need to help people," she says. "But that's the hardest thing to get: We're just the help, we're not the answer."

Doctors who are most comfortable saying "I don't know" tend to describe their relationships with patients as collaborative: They work together to assemble information and decide how to proceed. The doctor has the specialized knowledge; the patient presents the goal or need. In this paradigm, the doctor isn't entirely unlike a reference librarian helping a patron with a research project.

My friend Stokley happens to be a reference librarian. He works at the Evergreen State College, and saying "I don't know" is a big part of his job. In fact, it's what got him the job.

His initial interview was conducted over speakerphone. The head of the search committee asked, "What would you do if a student came to you looking for information on the American sublime?"

"Well, first," said Stokley, "I'd tell the student I don't know anything about that."

From the other end of the line, laughter.

"But that's a connection," he went on. "We both don't know. That's a kind of intimacy. So, okay, I'd start by asking them questions. What interests you about the sublime? Why does it interest you? What do you already know about it? What do you think about what you know?"

His boss, Sara, remembers the interview well. Other candidates had replied to the same question with stock answers, displaying their knowledge by listing the standard databases they'd consult. "Stokley's response was the only one that focused on the student," Sara says. "I remember big smiles around the table. We were, like, 'We found him. We can hang up now.'"

He started working the evening shift, and soon met and exceeded Sara's hopes by regularly calling her at home. She laughs, explaining: "I've trained so many people and I've always said, 'Call me if you have a question.' Stokley's literally the only person ever to do it. The first time he called—I was so happy! What a gift. What a *relief*. I thought: *Here's a person who knows how to take care of himself, to ask for help. He's a real grown-up.* It instills confidence."

Isn't that funny? Isn't it beautifully antithetical to what we go around fearing? Stokley's saying "I don't know," far from diminishing him in the eyes of others, *confirmed* his strength, his maturity, his capability. Not only that, it extends the possibilities for his connecting with others—with his boss and colleagues and also with library patrons, those students and faculty members who come bearing the dual gift of their own desires and limitations.

I don't know

In journalism school, I'd been afraid to admit I didn't know what a nut graf was because I dreaded exposing myself as inadequate. But the deeper dread was that I'd be cast off, abandoned, that a connection would be revoked. Consider the irony. We swallow the words "I don't know" for fear of rupture: The admission might sever us from those we love or esteem. But the passive lie—the pretense of knowing—causes shame: an internal rupture, a rupture of self. And the bond we think we've managed to sustain with others is not a real bond; it's based on falsity.

Now consider the alternative. We allow the words "I don't know" to fly from our mouths, perhaps as a confession of ignorance, perhaps as a voicing of uncertainty. Either way, the result is a relinquishing of control. We declare ourselves open to receiving information, ideas, and perspectives from beyond the borders of self. And in so doing, our connection to others and to the world is not ruptured. On the contrary. In the honest flow of giving and receiving, we are closer than ever.

So much becomes possible when we honor doubt.

. . .

What if we were to embrace saying "I don't know"? What if we were to see it as an instrument for opening up and extending all sorts of possibilities, including, crucially, the possibility for connections among people?

Our civic life is heavily marked—indeed, pocked—by debates in which each side is so certain of its position that any movement is effectively impossible. For that matter, *debate*—in its original sense of "to consider something, to deliberate"—is impossible. We wind up with so much sound and fury and nothing gained.

Only when we allow the possibility that we may not know for sure, when we slip out from under the terrible yoke of our own notions, when we shift from the fundamentalism that has hardened like clay around our feet and allow doubt to flow freely through our membranes—though this may sting— only in concert with such internal movement can meaningful external movement occur.

Take climate change. For years, scientists and advocates for responsible stewardship have been warning that climate change is a real and serious threat, largely caused by human behavior, and with the possibility of being mitigated or remedied by changes in human behavior. For years, big oil and others have been saying this is baloney. Despite the mounting evidence of global warming presented by scientists and advocates, the deniers seem unbudged. In fact, a 2012 study in the journal *Risk Analysis* shows a rise in global warming skepticism. (In 2002, only 7 percent of Americans had "naysayer associations," as opposed to more than 20 percent in 2010.)

One of the authors of that study, Anthony Leiserowitz, director of the Yale Project on Climate Change Communication, is a leading expert on the public's perception of climate change and the psychology of decision making. In a 2013 interview with Bill Moyers, he spoke to the issue of moving dialogue forward when both sides have entrenched points of view.

> **Bill Moyers**: Assume that I'm a skeptic. Not only a skeptic, but a Tea Party Republican who goes to church every Sunday where my beloved pastor tells me that, reassures me that God created the earth six thousand

years ago and that if God wants to end the
earth, God will on God's terms, that this
is out of our control. If you were sitting
across from a good, disciplined believer
like that, what argument would you make
to me?

Anthony Leiserowitz: Well, the first thing
I would do is I would listen, I would really listen. Because I'd want to know really
what are the depths of, not just their concerns about this issue, but what are their
aspirations? What do they want for
their children? What do they want for
their grandchildren? What kind of com-
munity do they want to live in? What are
the values that really animate and motivate them?

He continues at some length, not presenting
facts or studies or data, but rather detailing the
kind of conversation he would hope to engage in, a
conversation about ethos and desire and common
ground. But did you notice the very first thing he
said? Moyers asked what he'd argue and Leisero-

witz said he'd listen. He'd come from a place of not knowing, as a way of connecting with the other.

Can you *imagine* if politicians were to adopt this style of debate? Just picture it: the presidential candidates at their podiums, or senators and members of Congress on the legislative floor. There they are, assembled to debate issues and policies, bills and provisions, and instead of trammeling and tromping over one another with their words, they turn to one another and listen, really listen.

We see another example of how deep listening can loosen up entrenched beliefs in the realm of gay marriage. Here, it's often a specific human connection that sparks a willingness to think fluidly. The connection might be as direct as having a son or daughter who is gay. In March 2013, after the Republican senator Rob Portman reversed his position on gay marriage, he spoke of how his son's coming out had been instrumental in shifting him from his previous convictions. "It allowed me to think of this issue from a new perspective," he told reporters, "and that's of a dad who loves his son a lot and wants him to have the same opportunities that his brother and sister would have." Portman's loving wishes for his own son allowed him to re-consider what he thought he knew.

But the connection that moves us can also be more subtle, less direct. One year earlier, when President Obama announced his support for gay marriage, he spoke of his "evolution" on the issue being influenced by various personal relationships. First he named relationships with friends, family, neighbors, and members of his own staff who were in "incredibly committed" same-sex relationships. But later in the interview he spoke of another con-nection that contributed to his shift:

> You know, Malia and Sasha, they've got friends whose parents are same-sex couples. And I—you know, there have been times where Michelle and I have been sittin' around the dinner table. And we've been talkin' and—about their friends and their parents. And Malia and Sasha would—it wouldn't dawn on them that somehow their friends' parents would be treated differently. It doesn't make sense to them. And—and frankly—that's the kind of thing that prompts—a change of per-spective.

I don't know

The change of perspective Obama talks about here wasn't motivated by wanting something—in this case, marriage equality—that would directly benefit his children. Instead, it was enabled simply by listening to the views of people he loves and values and respects.

Nor do you have to be related to someone in order to be changed by your connection; the transformation might even arise from a contentious relationship. In 2010, David Blankenhorn, the founder and president of the Institute for American Values, was a star witness in California's Proposition 8 trial, testifying against gay marriage. But in the summer of 2012, in a move that shocked his allies and even his own board members, he announced he was dropping his opposition in favor of an egalitarian pro-marriage agenda. In a 2012 radio interview, asked to address what led to his change of heart, Blankenhorn first speaks in broad, abstract terms: *a process of thinking, conversation, intellectual argument*, etc. But then he begins to talk about Jonathan Rauch, the journalist and activist in favor of gay marriage. Initially, their relationship was antagonistic, to say the least. ("I said many ugly things about him," Blankenhorn recalls.)

leah hager cohen

But over time, debate led to rapport, rapport to empathy, and empathy to doubt. Blankenhorn tells the interviewer:

> I don't want to get schmaltzy about it, but
> the truth is . . .
>
> But the truth is that I probably
> wouldn't have changed my mind without
> knowing Jonathan personally. You know,
> and I used to think, well, oh, gee, what a
> lame thing, you know, your friendships
> are influencing your thinking.
>
> But, I—you know, you build up a kind
> of barriers of belief in theory, and it keeps
> the other people out, and so you talk about
> them. You have theories about them. You can
> explain their lives to them, but you never
> really talk to them and see it from their point
> of view. So for me as this guy from the
> South, older guy, you know, hadn't known
> many gay people, so it was a meaningful
> thing. And after [my] being very aggressive
> and abusive, you know, he responded with
> kindness and, like, uh, well, you know,
> maybe we could talk a little bit.

Maybe we could talk a little bit. The same thing Anthony Leiserowitz proposes. The same thing that happened between Rob Portman and his son. The same thing that happened around the Obama family dinner table. The same thing we are all capable of choosing, on a daily basis, with those people in our lives whom we do not fully fathom. Real civil discourse necessarily leaves room for doubt. This doesn't make us wishy-washy! We can still hold fervent beliefs. The difference is, we don't let those beliefs calcify into unconsidered doctrine. As Blankenhorn has written:

> *Doubt* and *civility* go together naturally, like ham and eggs, coffee and cream . . . Doubt is my friend. I don't mean that I've stopped having beliefs, or stopped being passionate about those beliefs; it's just that I'm more and more certain, when it comes to the free life of the mind, of the importance of uncertainty.

Human connection helps usher in doubt. Doubt may in turn increase the quality and reach of human connection. Put another way: In the presence of love we may soften our certainties, and

leah hager cohen

in the softening of our certainties we may be led into fuller love.

By the same logic, fundamentalism of any kind is the refusal to allow doubt. The opposite of fundamentalism is the willingness to say "I don't know."

But how frightening those words remain. Even if we can be persuaded that they do not commit us to loneliness or exile from human company, instead paving the way for more intimate, authentic connection, still they persist in reminding us of our essential vulnerability. We are small, limited creatures in an illimitable, unknowable world, appallingly wobbly beneath our feet.

Developmental psychologists say fear of the unknown presents in infants as young as five months. Evolutionary psychologists say such fear may be a positive adaptive behavior, one that helped early hominids avoid danger. But fear of the unknown is not quite identical to fear of not knowing. With the former, the peril is external. With the latter, it's rooted in the precincts of the self. The recognition that we are in some profound sense alone and without answers fills us with existential dread. Yet looked at another way, the realization may brim with hopeful possibility. The British psychoanalyst D. W. Winnicott called doubts about the self a "child's most sacred attribute." Whether we tilt more in the direction of dread or hope boils down to how we manage our feelings about living with mystery.

Primitive cultures responded to the unbearable scariness of mystery with a method at once simple and ingenious: What they didn't know, they made up. Why does it get dark at night? Because so many birds fill the sky, their wings block out the sun (so said the Mamaiurans of Brazil). Why has the moon been growing smaller? Because the gods have been imbibing some of its elixir (so said Hindu mythology). Why are all the people of my village getting sick? Because the god Tlaloc threw one of his wrathful lightning bolts our way (so said the Aztecs). And what, oh what, is that amazing ribbon of colored light arcing across the sky, making me weep and laugh and quiver with awe? That's Bifröst, said the ancient Norse: a shimmering bridge to Asgard, home of the gods.

In modern times we are no less anxious about the unknown, but we are more likely to seek comfort through science or ideology. Or, failing that, superstition. As a child, I went through an intense period of fearing the unknown. It affected me most upsettingly at bedtime, and for the better part of a year I could not go to sleep without the soothing relief of rituals that presented themselves to me without my consciously devising them: I became prisoner to a certain way of wrapping my head in the bedsheet, of rubbing my feet together, of silent counting and of matching my inhalations and exhalations to the rhythm of the numbers as I spoke them in my head.

I was helped to outgrow this phase by my mother, who one day invited me to sit at the kitchen table with pencil and paper and write down my fears. Of course, in order to do that, I had to give them language, and this minor intervention—the act of plucking them from the roiling stew of the unnameable and setting them down as words on lined paper, in my own familiar handwriting—tamed them somewhat.

The other, mightier, part of my recovery also came to me through my mother, but it took the exact opposite approach: Instead of an attempt to master my fears by coming to know them, it involved making friends with the unknown. My mother was not religious in any conventional sense, but she had a kind of faith in, and reverence for, that which must always remain mysterious. The way she opened herself up to this mystery without ever expecting to decrypt it conferred on me a sense of limitless potential and peace.

My mother held with no catechism, no rote set of questions and answers. She did not look to accrue knowledge pearls or put uncertainties to rest. She liked puzzles—crossword, jigsaw, tangram— and paper craft, and she liked making things with leaf and vine, thread and charcoal and yarn. Silver blades and matte board. Paint and cloth and wax. It seemed to me she'd spend forever rearranging things, feeling her way toward large patterns, toward harmonies of meaning and shape, but always with a looseness, an attentiveness to alteration. I remember watching her work at the kitchen table, wondering at her stern concentration, which at the time seemed almost a scowl, but which I now understand was a look of bottomless receptivity. A harking.

About death, that most intractable of mysteries, she was unrepining, curious, patient. The winter my oldest child was ten, he became frightened of death. He'd been sledding on a hill near home when his toboggan skimmed out of control, going much too fast for me to intercept him before he reached the road. There were no cars. He shot over the empty street and up the driveway opposite, smashing into a garage door which had been left open a foot. His toboggan continued into the garage; he was stopped at the point of contact between the garage door and his shin. There were tears, and the gash on his leg was already swelling, but no serious damage had been done.

That night in bed, he said he couldn't stop replaying the crash in his mind. He'd overheard a remark one of the grown-ups had made, something to the effect that if the garage door had been open another foot, "he might have been beheaded." That frightening phrase was now lodged in his imagination, compounding his fear of the concrete—a decapitating blow—with fear of the unthinkable—death.

Several days later we visited my parents. The

specter of death had been hovering over him for days, rattling his mood, interfering with his sleep, and now he spoke of it to my mother. She asked, "Did I ever tell you my theory about the contract?"

He shook his head.

"The way I think of it," she said, "is when we're born, we get this wonderful prize, we get to be a person in the world. We get to partake of life. There's only one condition: At some point we have to die. That's the contract."

The way she saw it, she continued, problems arise when people forget that dying is part of the contract all along. Problems arise when we fall into the trap of thinking death is unnatural. If we accept it as the single condition for receiving the vast, tremendous experience of being alive, if we keep this contract in mind, it can lift the dread. "I think it's a great deal," she said, with a kind of marveling happiness. This was about a year after she'd learned she was dying of cancer.

To regard the ultimate unknown as something not evil, not alarming or wrong, but just that: unknown. This was a gift she had to give.

.   .   .

Sometimes we bite our tongues rather than admit, "I don't know." This act arises from shame, and perpetuates shame, and is a shame. Other times we say "I don't know" in an effort to absolve ourselves of responsibility and vulnerability. This act borders on blasphemy. For when we use these words to ratify responsibility and embrace vulnerability, saying and thinking and feeling them become a form of grace.

Of course, it is possible to revel in the experience of not knowing without speaking a single word.

It's funny that my son's dread of dying arose from an experience with snow, for my mother loved snow with an ardor that bordered on the devout. She once copied down a line from a Billy Collins poem—*This is the true religion, the religion of snow*—and thumbtacked it to a corkboard. Snow, for her, was the universe's magnum opus, the icing on the cake, though in truth she thrilled to all weather, the very fact of it—its uncontrollable nature, its magisterial indifference, its inexhaustible mysteriousness. She passed along that devotion, that reverence for something we may never hope to master or comprehend, to us, her family. The most memorable lesson she ever gave me about falling willingly, in gratitude, toward the unknown was delivered without fanfare, without words, amid snow.

I was nine. School had been canceled because of a blizzard the night before. In the afternoon, my mother and I visited the library one town over. When we'd had our fill of books, my mother made a proposal: How about, instead of calling my father for a ride home, we walk? Four and a half miles north along the Hudson; it seemed to me not just far but far-fetched—and irresistible.

The snow had resumed falling, very lightly. Specks of glitter. There was the cold spangling our lungs, our breath hanging tinsel-like in front of our mouths, the faint dusky drum skin of the sky blackening over our heads. We hardly spoke. We walked and walked. Home was far off, and night deepened, and the land was foreign and huge. The lights in the houses along the road came on one by one, amber lozenges cut out of the darkness. Beyond the houses the river ran sluggish with ice. Streetlights shone and trees formed a vaulted ceiling above, with the white plumage of the pines splendid as arms, and the bony branches of the hardwoods like stained glass windows framing the beyond, and every twig encased in ice, glittering, celebrated, every single one: oh the world, the world, exquisitely insoluble.

GRATITUDE

This little book began as an even littler essay. It appeared on *Cognoscenti*, the online ideas and opinions page of WBUR, an affiliate of National Public Radio. I am grateful to the staff who supported it there: Iris Adler, program manager; Robin Lubbock, director of social media; and especially Frannie Carr Toth, editor and producer, without whose gentle, expert badgering over the course of several months I never would have written the piece. My stumbling block was the name: *cognoscenti* is Italian for "those in the know," and when first invited to contribute, all I could think was, "But I'm *not*." Of course, this reaction eventually yielded my subject.

I am equally grateful to my editor, Sarah McGrath, and my agent, Barney Karpfinger, for suggesting, once the essay went live, that there might be a book in it. I privately thought they were nuts. But as I began reporting, I found myself captivated by what seemed to be the swiftly multiplying facets of the topic. What a pleasure this has been. I am grateful, too, to everyone at the Karpfinger Agency and Riverhead who spotted long before I did that this could work, and who lent their expertise to making it work better: Cathy Jaque, Marc Jaffee, Kate Hurley, Sarah Stein, and Geoff Kloske.

Above all, thanks very much to everyone who granted me an interview. I ran out of space in which to include all the excellent stories you generously shared, but every single conversation informed the book in some valuable way, whether by providing leads, suggesting new lines of inquiry, interestingly reframing some aspect of the theme, or otherwise contributing to my understanding of what it means to say "I don't know."